Password & Organi...

This book belongs to

_____

All right reserved. This book or any portion thereof may not be reproduced or used in any manner whatsoever without the express written permission from the publisher.

Website URL	
Username Login	
Password	
Hint/Question	
Email	
Primary Use	

Notes: _____

_____

_____

_____

Website URL	
Username Login	
Password	
Hint/Question	
Email	
Primary Use	

Notes: _____

_____

_____

_____

Website URL	
Username Login	
Password	
Hint/Question	
Email	
Primary Use	

Notes: _____

_____

_____

Website URL	
Username Login	
Password	
Hint/Question	
Email	
Primary Use	

Notes: _____

_____

_____

Website URL	
Username Login	
Password	
Hint/Question	
Email	
Primary Use	

Notes: _____

_____

_____

_____

Website URL	
Username Login	
Password	
Hint/Question	
Email	
Primary Use	

Notes: _____

_____

_____

_____

Website URL	
Username Login	
Password	
Hint/Question	
Email	
Primary Use	

Notes: _____

_____

_____

_____

Website URL	
Username Login	
Password	
Hint/Question	
Email	
Primary Use	

Notes: _____

_____

_____

_____

Website URL	
Username Login	
Password	
Hint/Question	
Email	
Primary Use	

Notes: _____

_____

_____

Website URL	
Username Login	
Password	
Hint/Question	
Email	
Primary Use	

Notes: _____

_____

_____

Website URL	
Username Login	
Password	
Hint/Question	
Email	
Primary Use	

Notes: _____

_____

_____

_____

Website URL	
Username Login	
Password	
Hint/Question	
Email	
Primary Use	

Notes: _____

_____

_____

_____

Website URL	
Username Login	
Password	
Hint/Question	
Email	
Primary Use	

Notes: _____

_____

_____

_____

Website URL	
Username Login	
Password	
Hint/Question	
Email	
Primary Use	

Notes: _____

_____

_____

_____

Website URL	
Username Login	
Password	
Hint/Question	
Email	
Primary Use	

Notes: _____

_____

_____

Website URL	
Username Login	
Password	
Hint/Question	
Email	
Primary Use	

Notes: _____

_____

_____

Website URL	
Username Login	
Password	
Hint/Question	
Email	
Primary Use	

Notes: _____

_____

_____

_____

Website URL	
Username Login	
Password	
Hint/Question	
Email	
Primary Use	

Notes: _____

_____

_____

_____

Website URL	
Username Login	
Password	
Hint/Question	
Email	
Primary Use	

Notes: _____

_____

_____

_____

Website URL	
Username Login	
Password	
Hint/Question	
Email	
Primary Use	

Notes: _____

_____

_____

_____

Website URL	
Username Login	
Password	
Hint/Question	
Email	
Primary Use	

Notes: _____

_____

_____

Website URL	
Username Login	
Password	
Hint/Question	
Email	
Primary Use	

Notes: _____

_____

_____

Website URL	
Username Login	
Password	
Hint/Question	
Email	
Primary Use	

Notes: _____

_____

_____

_____

Website URL	
Username Login	
Password	
Hint/Question	
Email	
Primary Use	

Notes: _____

_____

_____

_____

Website URL	
Username Login	
Password	
Hint/Question	
Email	
Primary Use	

Notes: _____

_____

_____

_____

Website URL	
Username Login	
Password	
Hint/Question	
Email	
Primary Use	

Notes: _____

_____

_____

_____

Website URL	
Username Login	
Password	
Hint/Question	
Email	
Primary Use	

Notes: _____

_____

_____

Website URL	
Username Login	
Password	
Hint/Question	
Email	
Primary Use	

Notes: _____

_____

_____

Website URL	
Username Login	
Password	
Hint/Question	
Email	
Primary Use	

Notes: _____

_____

_____

_____

Website URL	
Username Login	
Password	
Hint/Question	
Email	
Primary Use	

Notes: _____

_____

_____

_____

Website URL	
Username Login	
Password	
Hint/Question	
Email	
Primary Use	

Notes: _____

_____

_____

Website URL	
Username Login	
Password	
Hint/Question	
Email	
Primary Use	

Notes: _____

_____

_____

Website URL	
Username Login	
Password	
Hint/Question	
Email	
Primary Use	

Notes: _____

_____

_____

Website URL	
Username Login	
Password	
Hint/Question	
Email	
Primary Use	

Notes: _____

_____

_____

Website URL	
Username Login	
Password	
Hint/Question	
Email	
Primary Use	

Notes: _____

_____

_____

_____

Website URL	
Username Login	
Password	
Hint/Question	
Email	
Primary Use	

Notes: _____

_____

_____

_____

Website URL	
Username Login	
Password	
Hint/Question	
Email	
Primary Use	

Notes: _____

_____

_____

Website URL	
Username Login	
Password	
Hint/Question	
Email	
Primary Use	

Notes: _____

_____

_____

Website URL	
Username Login	
Password	
Hint/Question	
Email	
Primary Use	

Notes: _____

_____

_____

Website URL	
Username Login	
Password	
Hint/Question	
Email	
Primary Use	

Notes: _____

_____

_____

Website URL	
Username Login	
Password	
Hint/Question	
Email	
Primary Use	

Notes: _____

_____

_____

_____

Website URL	
Username Login	
Password	
Hint/Question	
Email	
Primary Use	

Notes: _____

_____

_____

_____

Website URL	
Username Login	
Password	
Hint/Question	
Email	
Primary Use	

Notes: _____

_____

_____

_____

Website URL	
Username Login	
Password	
Hint/Question	
Email	
Primary Use	

Notes: _____

_____

_____

_____

Website URL	
Username Login	
Password	
Hint/Question	
Email	
Primary Use	

Notes: _____

Website URL	
Username Login	
Password	
Hint/Question	
Email	
Primary Use	

Notes: _____

Website URL	
Username Login	
Password	
Hint/Question	
Email	
Primary Use	

Notes: _____

_____

_____

Website URL	
Username Login	
Password	
Hint/Question	
Email	
Primary Use	

Notes: _____

_____

_____

Website URL	
Username Login	
Password	
Hint/Question	
Email	
Primary Use	

Notes: _____

_____

_____

Website URL	
Username Login	
Password	
Hint/Question	
Email	
Primary Use	

Notes: _____

_____

_____

Website URL	
Username Login	
Password	
Hint/Question	
Email	
Primary Use	

Notes: _____

_____

_____

Website URL	
Username Login	
Password	
Hint/Question	
Email	
Primary Use	

Notes: _____

_____

_____

Website URL	
Username Login	
Password	
Hint/Question	
Email	
Primary Use	

Notes: _____

_____

_____

Website URL	
Username Login	
Password	
Hint/Question	
Email	
Primary Use	

Notes: _____

_____

_____

Website URL	
Username Login	
Password	
Hint/Question	
Email	
Primary Use	

Notes:

Website URL	
Username Login	
Password	
Hint/Question	
Email	
Primary Use	

Notes:

Website URL	
Username Login	
Password	
Hint/Question	
Email	
Primary Use	

Notes: _____

Website URL	
Username Login	
Password	
Hint/Question	
Email	
Primary Use	

Notes: _____

Website URL	
Username Login	
Password	
Hint/Question	
Email	
Primary Use	

Notes: _____

_____

_____

Website URL	
Username Login	
Password	
Hint/Question	
Email	
Primary Use	

Notes: _____

_____

_____

Website URL	
Username Login	
Password	
Hint/Question	
Email	
Primary Use	

Notes: _____

_____

_____

_____

Website URL	
Username Login	
Password	
Hint/Question	
Email	
Primary Use	

Notes: _____

_____

_____

_____

Website URL	
Username Login	
Password	
Hint/Question	
Email	
Primary Use	

Notes: _____

_____

_____

Website URL	
Username Login	
Password	
Hint/Question	
Email	
Primary Use	

Notes: _____

_____

_____

Website URL	
Username Login	
Password	
Hint/Question	
Email	
Primary Use	

Notes: _____

_____

_____

Website URL	
Username Login	
Password	
Hint/Question	
Email	
Primary Use	

Notes: _____

_____

_____

Website URL	
Username Login	
Password	
Hint/Question	
Email	
Primary Use	

Notes: _____

_____

_____

Website URL	
Username Login	
Password	
Hint/Question	
Email	
Primary Use	

Notes: _____

_____

_____

Website URL	
Username Login	
Password	
Hint/Question	
Email	
Primary Use	

Notes: _____

_____

_____

Website URL	
Username Login	
Password	
Hint/Question	
Email	
Primary Use	

Notes: _____

_____

_____

Website URL	
Username Login	
Password	
Hint/Question	
Email	
Primary Use	

Notes: _____

_____

_____

Website URL	
Username Login	
Password	
Hint/Question	
Email	
Primary Use	

Notes: _____

_____

_____

Website URL	
Username Login	
Password	
Hint/Question	
Email	
Primary Use	

Notes: _____

_____

_____

Website URL	
Username Login	
Password	
Hint/Question	
Email	
Primary Use	

Notes: _____

_____

_____

Website URL	
Username Login	
Password	
Hint/Question	
Email	
Primary Use	

Notes:

Website URL	
Username Login	
Password	
Hint/Question	
Email	
Primary Use	

Notes:

M

Website URL	
Username Login	
Password	
Hint/Question	
Email	
Primary Use	

Notes: _____

_____

_____

Website URL	
Username Login	
Password	
Hint/Question	
Email	
Primary Use	

Notes: _____

_____

_____

Website URL	
Username Login	
Password	
Hint/Question	
Email	
Primary Use	

Notes: _____

_____

_____

_____

Website URL	
Username Login	
Password	
Hint/Question	
Email	
Primary Use	

Notes: _____

_____

_____

_____

Website URL	
Username Login	
Password	
Hint/Question	
Email	
Primary Use	

Notes: _____

_____

_____

Website URL	
Username Login	
Password	
Hint/Question	
Email	
Primary Use	

Notes: _____

_____

_____

Website URL	
Username Login	
Password	
Hint/Question	
Email	
Primary Use	

Notes: _____

_____

_____

_____

Website URL	
Username Login	
Password	
Hint/Question	
Email	
Primary Use	

Notes: _____

_____

_____

_____

Website URL	
Username Login	
Password	
Hint/Question	
Email	
Primary Use	

Notes: _____

_____

_____

Website URL	
Username Login	
Password	
Hint/Question	
Email	
Primary Use	

Notes: _____

_____

_____

Website URL	
Username Login	
Password	
Hint/Question	
Email	
Primary Use	

Notes: _____

_____

_____

Website URL	
Username Login	
Password	
Hint/Question	
Email	
Primary Use	

Notes: _____

_____

_____

Website URL	
Username Login	
Password	
Hint/Question	
Email	
Primary Use	

Notes: _____

_____

_____

Website URL	
Username Login	
Password	
Hint/Question	
Email	
Primary Use	

Notes: _____

_____

_____

Website URL	
Username Login	
Password	
Hint/Question	
Email	
Primary Use	

Notes: _____

_____

_____

_____

Website URL	
Username Login	
Password	
Hint/Question	
Email	
Primary Use	

Notes: _____

_____

_____

_____

Website URL	
Username Login	
Password	
Hint/Question	
Email	
Primary Use	

Notes: _____

_____

_____

Website URL	
Username Login	
Password	
Hint/Question	
Email	
Primary Use	

Notes: _____

_____

_____

Website URL	
Username Login	
Password	
Hint/Question	
Email	
Primary Use	

Notes: _____

_____

_____

Website URL	
Username Login	
Password	
Hint/Question	
Email	
Primary Use	

Notes: _____

_____

_____

Website URL	
Username Login	
Password	
Hint/Question	
Email	
Primary Use	

Notes: _____

_____

_____

_____

Website URL	
Username Login	
Password	
Hint/Question	
Email	
Primary Use	

Notes: _____

_____

_____

_____

Website URL	
Username Login	
Password	
Hint/Question	
Email	
Primary Use	

Notes:

Website URL	
Username Login	
Password	
Hint/Question	
Email	
Primary Use	

Notes:

Website URL	
Username Login	
Password	
Hint/Question	
Email	
Primary Use	

Notes: _____

_____

_____

Website URL	
Username Login	
Password	
Hint/Question	
Email	
Primary Use	

Notes: _____

_____

_____

Website URL	
Username Login	
Password	
Hint/Question	
Email	
Primary Use	

Notes:

Website URL	
Username Login	
Password	
Hint/Question	
Email	
Primary Use	

Notes:

Website URL	
Username Login	
Password	
Hint/Question	
Email	
Primary Use	

Notes: _____

_____

_____

Website URL	
Username Login	
Password	
Hint/Question	
Email	
Primary Use	

Notes: _____

_____

_____

Website URL	
Username Login	
Password	
Hint/Question	
Email	
Primary Use	

Notes: _____

_____

_____

_____

Website URL	
Username Login	
Password	
Hint/Question	
Email	
Primary Use	

Notes: _____

_____

_____

_____

Website URL	
Username Login	
Password	
Hint/Question	
Email	
Primary Use	

Notes: _____

_____

_____

Website URL	
Username Login	
Password	
Hint/Question	
Email	
Primary Use	

Notes: _____

_____

_____

Website URL	
Username Login	
Password	
Hint/Question	
Email	
Primary Use	

Notes: _____

Website URL	
Username Login	
Password	
Hint/Question	
Email	
Primary Use	

Notes: _____

Website URL	
Username Login	
Password	
Hint/Question	
Email	
Primary Use	

Notes: _____

_____

_____

Website URL	
Username Login	
Password	
Hint/Question	
Email	
Primary Use	

Notes: _____

_____

_____

Website URL	
Username Login	
Password	
Hint/Question	
Email	
Primary Use	

Notes: _____

_____

_____

_____

Website URL	
Username Login	
Password	
Hint/Question	
Email	
Primary Use	

Notes: _____

_____

_____

_____

Website URL	
Username Login	
Password	
Hint/Question	
Email	
Primary Use	

Notes: _____

_____

_____

Website URL	
Username Login	
Password	
Hint/Question	
Email	
Primary Use	

Notes: _____

_____

_____

Website URL	
Username Login	
Password	
Hint/Question	
Email	
Primary Use	

Notes: _____

_____

_____

_____

Website URL	
Username Login	
Password	
Hint/Question	
Email	
Primary Use	

Notes: _____

_____

_____

_____

Website URL	
Username Login	
Password	
Hint/Question	
Email	
Primary Use	

Notes: _____

_____

_____

_____

Website URL	
Username Login	
Password	
Hint/Question	
Email	
Primary Use	

Notes: _____

_____

_____

_____

Website URL	
Username Login	
Password	
Hint/Question	
Email	
Primary Use	

Notes: _____

_____

_____

Website URL	
Username Login	
Password	
Hint/Question	
Email	
Primary Use	

Notes: _____

_____

_____

Website URL	
Username Login	
Password	
Hint/Question	
Email	
Primary Use	

Notes: _____

_____

_____

Website URL	
Username Login	
Password	
Hint/Question	
Email	
Primary Use	

Notes: _____

_____

_____

Website URL	
Username Login	
Password	
Hint/Question	
Email	
Primary Use	

Notes: _____

_____

_____

_____

Website URL	
Username Login	
Password	
Hint/Question	
Email	
Primary Use	

Notes: _____

_____

_____

_____

V

Website URL	
Username Login	
Password	
Hint/Question	
Email	
Primary Use	

Notes: _____

_____

_____

_____

Website URL	
Username Login	
Password	
Hint/Question	
Email	
Primary Use	

Notes: _____

_____

_____

_____

Website URL	
Username Login	
Password	
Hint/Question	
Email	
Primary Use	

Notes: _____

_____

_____

_____

Website URL	
Username Login	
Password	
Hint/Question	
Email	
Primary Use	

Notes: _____

_____

_____

_____

Website URL	
Username Login	
Password	
Hint/Question	
Email	
Primary Use	

Notes: _____

_____

_____

Website URL	
Username Login	
Password	
Hint/Question	
Email	
Primary Use	

Notes: _____

_____

_____

Website URL	
Username Login	
Password	
Hint/Question	
Email	
Primary Use	

Notes: _____

_____

_____

Website URL	
Username Login	
Password	
Hint/Question	
Email	
Primary Use	

Notes: _____

_____

_____

Website URL	
Username Login	
Password	
Hint/Question	
Email	
Primary Use	

Notes: _____

_____

_____

Website URL	
Username Login	
Password	
Hint/Question	
Email	
Primary Use	

Notes: _____

_____

_____

Website URL	
Username Login	
Password	
Hint/Question	
Email	
Primary Use	

Notes: _____

_____

_____

_____

Website URL	
Username Login	
Password	
Hint/Question	
Email	
Primary Use	

Notes: _____

_____

_____

_____

Website URL	
Username Login	
Password	
Hint/Question	
Email	
Primary Use	

Notes: _____

_____

_____

Website URL	
Username Login	
Password	
Hint/Question	
Email	
Primary Use	

Notes: _____

_____

_____

Website URL	
Username Login	
Password	
Hint/Question	
Email	
Primary Use	

Notes:

Website URL	
Username Login	
Password	
Hint/Question	
Email	
Primary Use	

Notes:

Website URL	
Username Login	
Password	
Hint/Question	
Email	
Primary Use	

Notes: _____

_____

_____

Website URL	
Username Login	
Password	
Hint/Question	
Email	
Primary Use	

Notes: _____

_____

_____

Website URL	
Username Login	
Password	
Hint/Question	
Email	
Primary Use	

Notes: _____

_____

_____

Website URL	
Username Login	
Password	
Hint/Question	
Email	
Primary Use	

Notes: _____

_____

_____

Website URL	
Username Login	
Password	
Hint/Question	
Email	
Primary Use	

Notes: _____

_____

_____

Website URL	
Username Login	
Password	
Hint/Question	
Email	
Primary Use	

Notes: _____

_____

_____

Website URL	
Username Login	
Password	
Hint/Question	
Email	
Primary Use	

Notes: _____

_____

_____

_____

Website URL	
Username Login	
Password	
Hint/Question	
Email	
Primary Use	

Notes: _____

_____

_____

_____

Website URL	
Username Login	
Password	
Hint/Question	
Email	
Primary Use	

Notes: _____

_____

_____

_____

Website URL	
Username Login	
Password	
Hint/Question	
Email	
Primary Use	

Notes: _____

_____

_____

_____

Website URL	
Username Login	
Password	
Hint/Question	
Email	
Primary Use	

Notes: _____

_____

_____

_____

Website URL	
Username Login	
Password	
Hint/Question	
Email	
Primary Use	

Notes: _____

_____

_____

_____

This page intentionally left blank

Printed in Great Britain
by Amazon